HOLY SPIRIT
INSPIRED POEMS

HOLY SPIRIT INSPIRED POEMS

Kier Collins

Xulon Press

Xulon Press
2301 Lucien Way #415
Maitland, FL 32751
407.339.4217
www.xulonpress.com

© 2023 by Kier Collins

All rights reserved solely by the author. The author guarantees all contents are original and do not infringe upon the legal rights of any other person or work. No part of this book may be reproduced in any form without the permission of the author.

Due to the changing nature of the Internet, if there are any web addresses, links, or URLs included in this manuscript, these may have been altered and may no longer be accessible. The views and opinions shared in this book belong solely to the author and do not necessarily reflect those of the publisher. The publisher therefore disclaims responsibility for the views or opinions expressed within the work.

Unless otherwise indicated, Scripture quotations taken from the New American Standard Bible (NASB). Copyright © 1960, 1962, 1963, 1968, 1971, 1972, 1973, 1975, 1977, 1995 by The Lockman Foundation. Used by permission. All rights reserved.

Scripture quotations taken from the Amplified Bible (AMP). Copyright © 2015 by The Lockman Foundation. Used by permission. All rights reserved.

Scripture quotations taken from the English Standard Version (ESV). Copyright © 2001 by Crossway, a publishing ministry of Good News Publishers. Used by permission. All rights reserved.

Scripture quotations taken from the King James Version (KJV)–public domain.

Paperback ISBN-13: 978-1-66288-320-0
Ebook ISBN-13: 978-1-66288-321-7

Acknowledgment to those who inspired me to write the poems and to those who encouraged me to share them with the world:

Kat Kerr
Donna Rigney
Jalen Wilson
Robin Bullock
Ken Johnson (Th.D)
Kieran the Light
Marcus Rogers
Curtis Browne
Wesley Waites
Granny June

A special thanks to my gran June, your love of poetry may have skipped a generation but it lives on in me. I look forward to seeing you again, one of the first things we'll have to do when I make it up there is have a game of golf!

> *So they got up early in the morning and went out into the wilderness of Tekoa; and as they went out, Jehoshaphat stood and said, "Hear me, O Judah, and you inhabitants of Jerusalem! Believe and trust in the Lord your God and you will be established (secure). Believe and trust in His prophets and succeed."*
>
> 2 Chronicles 20:20 (AMP)

Table of Contents

1. The Prodigal Son 1
2. Keep Pushing Forward 2
3. My Heart Aches 3
4. Bearing the Pain 4
5. This Life Is the Seed 5
6. A Host Beyond All Reckoning 6
7. An Eternal Life More Real 7
8. Comfort in His Loving Tether 8
9. Until Daylight Is Claimed Back 9
10. This Life, The Next 10
11. The First Adam to the Last 12
12. He Foreknew Our Pain 13
13. We Rest Safely in the Palm 15
14. Winter Passed Away 16
15. Eternity Is Calling Me 17
16. The Road Less Travelled 19
17. A Moment of Clarity 20
18. All Creation Groans in Expectation 22
19. The Whisperings of the World 24
20. Divine Invitation 26
21. Love like Boys and Girls 27
22. Transitory by Nature 28
23. The Grace of God 29
24. The Bridegroom Is Delaying 30
25. Until the Final Trumpet Sounds 32
26. The Time Is at Hand 34
27. He Will Wipe Away All Tears 36
28. A 2000 Year Old Promise of Hope 38
29. A Small Part to Play 40
30. A Mystery with a Simple Complexion 42

31. The Answers I Do Not Know 44
32. It Lifts Me Up to Heights Unseen. 46
33. Giver of Imperishable Treasure 49
34. We Will Look into His Eyes 51
35. Never Again Subject to Sin 53
36. We Are All Guilty 55
37. I Know the Wait Is Worth It 57
38. Thank You Lord for Changing My Heart 59
39. Accept His Love and Sacrifice. 61
40. Faith, Hope and Love 62
41. Love Your Neighbour as Yourself 63
42. Through Toils and Terrors 65
43. Find Your Gift and It Will Pay. 67
44. He left His Kingly Estate 69
45. We Are Claiming Back the Darkness. 70
46. The Earth Needs Healing 72
47. The Sovereign Soul-Saver 74
48. Take Control of Your Vessel. 75
49. He Is Your Maker. 77
50. Our God Is The King 78
51. An Inbuilt Persistence 80
52. In This Festive Season 82
53. The Joy Of The Lord Is Your Strength. 84
54. For He Himself Is Our Peace 85
55. As In the Days of Noah 86
56. Satan Will Suffer the Last Defeat 88
57. Seek Peace and Pursue It. 89
58. In a World of War and Greed. 91
59. King of Kings. 92
60. Kings, Priests and Prophets 93
61. The Earth Is His Footstool. 94
62. What Has Been Before 95
63. Joe Biden Will Fall. 96
64. Jesus Will See Us Through 97

65. God Is the Referee 98
66. Children of Light 99
67. What You Enter Into 100
68. Everything Changes Through Jesus 101
69. No Longer in Bondage 102
70. Lord, Send Your Fire 103
71. I Am With You Always 104
72. A Father of the Fatherless 105
73. For He Is Coming. 106
74. The Only Way to Be Victorious 107
75. He Created the Stars. 108
76. If God Let Everyone Go to Heaven 109
77. Observe How the Trees Grow 110
78. But Take Courage 111
79. He Created Us. 112
80. How Blessed Is the Man 113
81. All Can Be Set Free. 114
82. The Lord Waits 115
83. Haman Paid the King 116
84. His Arms Wide Open. 117
85. Our Father and Adonai 118
86. My Father's Business 119
87. Pharaoh Was Just a Man 120
88. Every Need Provided For 121
89. The World Is Being Shaken. 122
90. A Difficult Paradox 123
91. This Is the Essence of True Love 124
92. Ascending the Eternal Staircase 125
93. Don't Give Up 126
94. Pass Through Life's Trials. 127
95. All The Mysteries of God to Reveal. 128
96. Glory to God 129
97. The Fullness Thereof. 130
98. The Hour Is Now 131

99. The Prince of Peace 132
100. He Restores My Soul. 133
101. Won't Stop Singing 135
102. A Time to Reap 136
103. Get in the Word 137
104. Eternal Source of Bliss 138
105. Sword of the Spirit 140
106. No House Divided 142
107. The Mysteries of God. 143
108. Glory to Jesus 146
109. All Flesh and Bone. 147
110. The Day Will Come 149
111. Lined With Pearls 151
112. The Ground Shakes 152
113. Every Deed Recorded 153
114. A Day Is Coming. 155
115. Rightful Positions 157
116. Love Has a Face 158
117. He Is the Only Way 160
118. A New Reality Looming 162
119. The Glorious King 164
120. The Cross of Christ 166
121. The Triumphal Entry. 168
122. I Will Be Ready 170
123. Love Is Patient. 172
124. All The World Will See 174
125. The New Reality. 176
126. Meditate in Your Heart 178
127. Never Stood a Chance 179
128. Nothing Will Stay The Same 180
129. Deliver Me From Fantasy 181
130. A Lush Green Valley. 183

The Prodigal Son

The prodigal son.
My heart is overcome.
Years in the wilderness,
It was me who willed it.

He has called me home.
I was never alone.
The mind plays tricks,
That is satan's wish.

No man is an island
Adrift at sea,
That was me.
Newfound fellowship.
Christ shows me how to see.

He has called me home.
A change of heart was needed;
With God my soul pleaded.
A thorn in the side;
His grace keeps me alive.

Keep Pushing Forward

The day is young.
The night will end.
Keep pushing forward.
In time He will commend.

The depth of man.
The pulsing of his heart.
The journey of his soul;
Skyward it will depart.

A global ancestral lobotomy,
Big pharma says healthy… It must be!
Only interested in the money,
A fabricated man-made cacophony.

The Western world pays to heal,
Chinese tradition only if you are healed.
A society dependant on pills,
'It's all OK I'm up to date with my bills.'

In this fast paced world of wealth,
A frequent after thought is our state of health.
We only get one body,
May we preserve it through taming our folly.

My Heart Aches

My heart aches.
My soul must wait.
My heavenly king,
My mouth ought to sing.

Your might and power.
Your beauty as of choicest flower.
Your patience globally known;
Your loving-kindness all will know.

My time shall come.
My emotions will be overcome.
My fleeting life;
My purpose, to spread your light.

Your holy name.
Your glory knows no shame.
Your suffering and pain.
Your love exhorts I change.

My heart aches.
My soul must wait.
My heavenly king,
It is to you my mouth will sing.

Bearing the Pain

The anguish of pain,
Just know He took the blame.
An unrelenting thorn in the side,
His righteous judgement.
His grace keeps me alive.

The question of suffering,
For some long, for some short.
An existential fact,
Rife throughout humanity's past.

He suffered and sacrificed.
He will remove the notion of night.
Sent of the Father's will;
The sanctifying propitiation
Offered up on that hill.

What an honor and a privilege
To share in His pain;
To remain faithful throughout the struggle
Undoubtedly leads to gain.

We all share in His body.
We all share in this world.
May we remain faithful until the end.
We will be overwhelmed with joy,
When the host of heaven descend.

This Life Is the Seed

Seventy years or eighty if due to strength.
A repetitive cycle to sin then repent.
New trends and new technologies;
A new wheel for mankind,
No need to reinvent.

A thousand years here,
A thousand years there;
A mere day to the Lord.
For our soul's salvation He cares.

Love can be kind,
Love may seem harsh,
Is it not love to let one suffer?
If you know it will strengthen their mind.

This life is the seed,
A gift from He who sows.
Everyday an opportunity,
For our soul to grow and grow.

A Host Beyond All Reckoning

"The grass withers,
The flower fades;"
But the word of He most gracious
Shall surpass the end of days.

The fading of the sun,
The setting of a dream.
A host beyond all reckoning,
A sight soon to be seen.

Origin and meaning,
Morality and destiny.
Inbuilt questions,
Left to ponder, until the righteous insurrection.

"In whom are hidden all the treasures of wisdom and knowledge."
"If anyone keeps my word, he will never taste death."
Transitory mortals,
Who are we to put our God to the test?

A love beyond all measure,
A love beyond all reason.
His tender love and care,
Will see us through this season.

Scripture referenced: Isaiah 40:8, Colossians 2:3, John 8:52 (ESV)

An Eternal Life More Real

A slave to sin.
Mortality this life does underpin.
The very air He breathes,
I am not worthy to share with Him.

Going out on a limb.
The wisest human minds
Conspiring to shape these times,
No limb needed with hope in the King.

We are the fleshly alabaster,
Moulded by the heavenly Master.
Humanity's pace has quickened.
If I could have been there,
Oh how His face would have glistened.

From time immemorial,
An eternal life more real.
The guiding hand of this existence.
To strive for the stars an inbuilt persistence.

They glisten and gleam
Yet the light not their own.
They and all their host;
A gift from the sovereign One,
Seated on His heavenly throne.

Comfort in His Loving Tether

To climb the stairway,
No longer a castaway.
To accept the gracious gift.
Eternal relief from dismay.

To see the heavens,
To soar the sky,
To ascend beyond gathered clouds.
Incredulous to that phrase goodbye.

Higher than an eagles feather.
Comfort in His loving tether.
What a peaceful feeling,
It will last forever…

Silent praise,
A chordless song,
An implicit partaking
In the eternal throng.

The choicest flower.
The mightiest king's power.
A mere breath or worthless breeze,
Compared to certain glory
On display in that final hour.

Until Daylight Is Claimed Back

A fading light.
An enveloping gloom.
A skyline of fog,
I hope it clears soon.

The birds still chirp,
The birds still sing;
From their first day a work complete,
It is the aerodynamic wing.

The trees still grow,
The flowers still bloom.
The crisp cold air,
I hope it returns soon.

The sky's inhabitants,
Oh how they glide.
Come rain or snow,
Their dwelling remains on high.

The clocks shift forward,
The nights shift back.
Won't be long now,
Until daylight is claimed back.

This Life, the Next

This fleeting life,
The changing tide.
The destiny of man,
The world has tried to hide.

This fleeting life,
The changing tide.
A post-truth culture,
Disavowal of every kind.

At night time, luminescent airglow.
A single progeny far below.
From dust thou hast come,
To dust this form returns.

At night time, luminescent airglow.
A progeny swayed too and fro.
To seek truth,
The world no longer wants to know.

A whole generation,
A constant state of agitation.
Postmodernism, the valiant stance.
Naturalism, the cause of humanity's trance.

A whole generation,
A spiritual degradation.

No different to beast and fowl;
Easy fodder for the one who prowls.

An intrinsic worth.
Lessons to pain and hurt.
Are we just flesh and bone?
If so, why compassion for the poor that groan?

An intrinsic worth,
Made known through pain and hurt.
Unconditional love,
Allows suffering to attain immortality above.

Flesh and bone.
Water and spirit.
This life, the next,
Controlled by He who is perfect.

To seek man's glory,
An earthly story.
Seek the face of God above,
A task made easy through faith and love.

The First Adam to the Last

A graceful psalm.
A solemn song.
Irrespective of wordly pleasures
My spirit shall continue on.

A sunken treasure.
A sinful pleasure.
His Spirit I am gifted,
Will see me through this weather.

A hardened heart.
A pre-planned crime.
Disavowal of our immoral actions,
The zeitgeist of this waning time.

Those mighty men,
The men of renown;
When our Lord was done,
The world absent of their sound.

An age of grace.
The righteous souls still wait.
The first Adam to the last.
Faith, a test that all must pass.

HE FOREKNEW OUR PAIN

His pain filled story.
Our eternal glory.
'He is not the One,'
The Pharisees proclaimed so surely.

A caring father
Shares his child's hurt.
To live and die as one of us.
Now we know its worth.

Why this world?
Why this pain?
Why no suffering?
Doesn't He love us all the same?

If not this world,
Then it's not you.
That family tree,
A host entirely new.

'He is immoral,
He foreknew our pain,
And yet He allowed us
To come to be all the same.'

If this makes God immoral,
If it diminishes His care;

Then every parent is thus too,
Knowing a child will face some despair.

We Rest Safely in the Palm

The loftiest house.
The fairest Queen.
A mere moment in time,
To all that will be seen.

Store your wealth in heaven.
Save your soul from death below.
The temptations of this world,
Are a forceful undertow.

We need not despair,
Nor turn our backs on care.
We rest safely in the palm,
Of He most gracious and fair.

"Neither moth nor rust destroys."
A destined heavenly envoy.
All the opulence of this world below.
Nil. Nothing, when our rewards are bestowed.

Eternal treasures money cannot buy.
Eternal joy, at present hidden from our eyes.
Eternal peace bereft of blame.
Watching and waiting.
The King will come again.

Scripture referenced: Matthew 6:20

Winter Passed Away (Haiku)

Enveloping gloom.
Sullen sea of static cloud.
Summer cries out loud.

Warmth casts asunder.
Irrespective birds wonder,
Oh how long summer?

Winter passed away,
His remnant fades day by day.
Summer, don't delay.

Hiding sun no more.
Frozen beauty left earth's floor.
Life abounds again.

Blooming starts again.
Mating cycle starts again.
Frosty mornings end.

Eternity Is Calling Me

A variety of gifts
Yet only one Spirit.
A multitude of ministries
Yet only One who wills it.

I plead with you,
My brethren here today;
Please open your heart
And turn from dismay.

He is our King.
He is our God.
None can compare,
To the righteous One above.

Tears of joy,
The Lord has seen fit to employ.
The days to come,
Akin to the dream of a little boy.

We will live together.
We will live forever.
Not some dreamy fantasy
But a reality for you and me!

One year here,
Ten years next.

Holy Spirit Inspired Poems

The dreams of man,
They are complex.

Eternity is calling me.
Our wedding feast a joy to see.
Lift up your hearts,
Lift them up to the Lord;
The end of time – a rapturous applause.

The Road Less Travelled

The road less travelled is hard to find.
Prudence and patience will protect from haughty eyes.
Through many jungles and over many canyons;
The drive to continue on,
The choicest of companions.

Through many storms and seasons,
That reliable companion shall keep my life from ceasing.
Out for the count, I'm the only soul about.
Things could always be worse.
A multitude of opportunities,
Simply choose one and rehearse.

Not the desire of God you see,
For all to live in self-righteous poverty.
So used to a Western invention,
'Self-made worth warrants a monetary suspension.'

What happened to an honest days pay?
What happened to minding our own way?
Guilty until proven otherwise,
That will be this paradigm's demise.

A lack of love and trust.
Irrelevant television mostly filled with lust,
Thousands of adverts a day.
Let's not forget, each must find their own way.

A Moment of Clarity

A moment of clarity.
A cold and bleak disparity.
All for One and One for all,
The destiny of humanity.

Bleak but not belated.
The joy of life elevated.
Above all thought and feeling;
Peace rests within our meaning.

A slave to sin.
We will win.
The current zeitgeist of this time,
'We'll believe anything but Him.'

The worn out pages.
The gift to give
Oh how it's contagious.
Submit to the Rock of Ages.

The infallible One.
His heavenly throng.
Rejoice and sing,
We know it won't be long.

Resplendent light and sound.
Melted mountains, melted ground.

Peals of thunder, flashes of lightning.
A glorious revealing, oh so frightening.

All Creation Groans in Expectation

A blazing flame casts asunder.
Those haughty forces set to plunder.
Long-held mystery of name and place.
One thing for certain – the Lord will displace.

The beating drum of conflict sounds.
The eyes of the world look around.
An ancient tip-off given by He,
Ezekiel the chosen man,
It's within his prophecy.

One third of a life is an absurd price.
One third of a wife – a contentious life.
One third taken out leaves 666 to remain;
Why then regard one third of the bible with apathetic shame?

Times are coming.
Times will be soon.
He will not withhold His anger,
Much like the coming of a new moon.

Gog, Meshech and Tubal,
Will be guided by His hand.
"Thoughts will come into your mind
And you will devise an evil plan."

No worry or fear.
We will reign a thousand years.
Watching and waiting;
All creation groans in expectation.

Scripture referenced: Ezekiel 38:10

The Whisperings of the World

Emblazoned glory with light and sound;
The voice of the archangel reverberating through the ground.
A wide open valley and a fertile plain;
The armies of the earth never to be seen again.

The loftiest commander will be laid down low;
The final insurrection, get ready for the show.
Righteous judgment falls across the land.
The spirit of rebellion, there He shall confound.

The whisperings of the world starting down below.
Put on the full armor of God.
Break free from this undertow.
Who knows? This may be the last tomorrow.

Radiant light and peals of sound;
Sensory overload – glory seen, glory abounds.
The marching beat of myriads of feet;
Inescapably marching toward their last defeat.

They smell blood and they sense victory;
They say to themselves 'Aha! We shall overcome He.'
A grave misfortune and a dire miscalculation.
Have they not heard? "He will rule all nations."

A gracious gift to man far below.

Sanctified on the cross for all to know.
Seize immortality, forsake fleeting vanity.
Transitory by nature,
Nevertheless destined to shake hands with our Creator.

Scripture referenced: Revelation 19:15

Divine Invitation

I sit and gaze into the sky,
Pondering in awe,
How do birds so graciously fly?

The lone mavericks and the faithful friends,
Both travel the horizon,
A road that never ends.

Seasons come and seasons change.
No two days ever the same.

People laugh and people cry,
Some may never truly understand why.

We wish to love.
We wish to provide.
Always longing to feel alive.

The answer may invoke
A feeling of surprise;
All you have to do is let go
And welcome in the divine.

Love like Boys and Girls

Open your heart.
Relax your mind.
Clear to His elect,
We're still in the end times.

Some seek solitude.
Some scoffed for being prude.
Objective representation of ideas,
Hopelessly misconstrued.

The essence inside one and all,
Diametrically opposed to they that chose to fall.
The outstretched ladder to unseen ends.
Remain steadfast, in time He shall commend.

Landscape, sunlit haze.
Lovers of self, the latest craze.
Peace in numbered days?

The essence inside one and all.
A single progeny on this ball.
An endless battle to allay.
Hardened hearts will not escape.

Fortify the positions.
Rule this world.
What does man need most?
Love like boys and girls.

Transitory by Nature

Transitory by nature,
We easily forget who created us.
Wandering here and wandering there.
No strangers to despair.

The passage of time is unending,
New beginning after new beginning always pending.
Short and concise.
This life is subject to strife.

However we need not despair,
The fate of our future rests with One who is gracious and fair.
He wishes to ascribe us a sound mind.
Lest we forget, this life only lasts a short time.

All in all I hope that these words may console.
Just remember,
All of the worries of life
Are but a blink of an eye to the soul.

The Grace of God

God is gracious.
God is kind.
God is always on my mind.

From dusk til dawn.
From week to week.
God's mighty power will save the meek.

Open your heart.
Relax your mind.
Clear to His elect,
We are in the end times.

Human nature,
Internal traitor.
No one intentionally says,
'I'll treat you like a fleeting vapor.'

No intention,
Yet absent a loving intervention.
Fair to say we're all tired
Of the brainwashed media's intentions.

The Bridegroom Is Delaying

My God.
My love.
The highest King above.
Loftier than the highest tower.
I pray to escape that final hour.

The radiance of your face,
Surpasses the beauty of even the choicest flower.
Dates come and dates go.
Man's transitory nature;
A yearning to know that which is reserved for our Creator.

A moments hesitation.
The bridegroom is delaying.
Faith of some wavering.

Not me oh Lord,
May it never be.
Your promise and your gift still stand,
That is my destiny.
I hope that those meek of heart
Shall also be set free.

The confines of this mortal life;
Seventy or eighty years, no doubt filled with strife.

No ones better, no ones worse.

We all live in this wondrous universe.
Don't fixate on the material purse.
Come to understand your soul's worth!

An eternal gift to traverse heaven's skies.
From He that said,
"Their fire is never quenched and their worm never dies."

Scripture referenced: Mark 9:48

Until the Final Trumpet Sounds

I say this life is fleeting.
My heart will keep on beating;
Until the final trumpet sounds,
Then will I be free from the shackles of this ground.

To accomplish the goal of this life,
Seek the love of God and say no to strife.
There is a whole new world up there.
For material possessions it does not care.

Seize hold of immortality.
Let go of this mundane reality.
Faith, hope and love,
An endless source from up above.

He is our maker.
The eternal Creator.
Our purpose until the end of time,
To abide in His presence,
Where His eternal light will shine.

You are my brothers.
You are my sisters.
Call on the name of God.
He is the eternal gifter.

A love so pure.
A power so true.
I hope that someday soon
I'll be in heaven with you.

If only we could all turn from derision,
By acknowledging God-given precision.
No more ill-fated decisions.
Will you allow your soul to be imprisoned?

Look up to the sky then bow,
Clasp your hands together and make that sealing vow.
Honestly admit you're a sinner.
I promise you this,
In the end we will be winners.

The Time Is at Hand

Our Lord Jesus Christ,
He paid the ultimate price.
The time is at hand.
Will you holdfast to His commands?

Age to age.
Day to day.
The world is not meant to be this way.

The chosen few will be made ageless;
A gift from the One most courageous.
He is the Rock of Ages.
We will stand before God blameless.

Not for any deed or man-made creed,
But a gift from He who said,
"Behold, I am coming like a thief."

The world will stare in disbelief.
Many will remain unrepentant.
Yet for me and you a final abatement;
Abatement from a world we do not know,
Abatement from long-suffering and sorrow.

Wave goodbye to this life.
An eternity of wonder awaits me and you.
A gracious throng transitioned from old to new.

Hear me now and take strength from these words.
From the young to the old,
The timid to the bold.

"Do not quench the Spirit."
Instead fill it,
Fill it to the brim.
Maintain faith and hope for all that He will bring.

"Behold, I am making all things new."
If you are of like mind I will meet you.
Praise His name.
Love those who delight in another's shame.
Me and you will never be the same.

The time is at hand.
There is only one plan.
Hold to that which is good.
Always be mindful,
You are being watched from up above.

Scripture referenced: Revelation 16:15, 1 Thessalonians 5:19, Revelation 21:5

He Will Wipe Away All Tears

One ruler above all,
He who judges the ones that fall.
The Son will arrive soon.
The heady of the body,
Giving signs in sun and moon.

I want to live in the world of tomorrow;
A world free from derision,
A world free from sorrow.

Faith, hope and love.
The New Jerusalem shall come down from up above.
Hold fast to what you have,
That is the good and not the bad.
No need longing for the past.

"He will wipe away all tears."
"We will reign with Christ a thousand years."
He does calm all our fears.

Take strength in the knowledge
Of a 2000 year old promise.
No longer a far away dream.
Soon He will be seen.

Seen first by the resurrected few,
Soon to follow will be me and you.

Together in the sky.
Soon we will wave this world goodbye.

Scripture referenced: Revelation 21:4, Revelation 20:4

A 2000 Year Old Promise of Hope

Our Lord Jesus Christ,
For us He paid the ultimate price.
Without measure giving the water of life.
We need only heed His advice.

"The Spirit and the bride say come,"
Sharing all truth until the battle is won.
We will live forever with He.
His grace and equity far beyond me.

A 2000 year old promise of hope,
Lest we begin to fade and become ghosts.
We are not empty inside.
Soon we will share in His prize.

Safe in His bosom forevermore;
We need only open our heart's door.
God's Holy Spirit rests within me;
I pray also that it is within thee.

No greater joy in this fleeting life,
Than to look up and know of His might.

Faith beyond measure.
An eternal wealth of treasure.
Simply lay aside the desire of the flesh;

A 2000 Year Old Promise of Hope

Speak to Jesus Christ and confess.

He will love us forevermore,
We need only open our heart's door.

Scripture referenced: Revelation 22:17

A Small Part to Play

The fading of the sun.
The setting of a dream.
A realm of awe and wonder,
A vision soon to be seen.

One Spirit and one Lord.
All will soon applaud.

The will of He that loves us,
More mighty than a mountain,
More beautiful than the clearest fountain.

To reside in the presence of the Father,
Many regard as hopeful chatter.
They will be held accountable.
The will of He who made us,
Is simply insurmountable.

The journey of the soul,
A never ending crescendo.
Break free from fleshly innuendos.
Where will its journey end?
Who can possibly know?

A small part to play.
Developing and growing everyday.
To seek peace and unity,

A desire deeply rooted in me.

Our individual souls,
Each a branch of the cosmic tree.
It's roots go down and deep,
The divine branches
Made up of those who are meek.

To speak the truth.
To encourage the weak.
By embracing both,
There can be no defeat.

A Mystery with a Simple Complexion

God is the rod,
Love is the line.
Every believer's soul is divine.

The seed of life and the passage of time,
A universal relationship
No man's will can unwind.

From the moment of conception,
Fast forward to our deathbed reflection.
Hopefully surrounded by all those who care,
No matter some will have minimal hair.

A human life is worth far more than its external appearance;
A jewel easily lost in this repetitive world of coherence.
To take comfort in a friend's presence.
To be satisfied with the simple pleasures.

Observing and learning can withhold the restless yearning;
A yearning for constant attention
Or cohering to the latest government invention.
A mystery with a simple complexion,
To be content in a moment of solitary reflection.
The mind is a stallion,
Intuition holds the reins.
Relentlessly ticking over,

Searching for those that think the same.

A search that can last a lifetime,
Inner peace a soul may never find.
An option for all to explore;
Simply slow down, relax,
And invite Jesus through your heart's door.

The Answers I Do Not Know

I sit and gaze into the evening sky,
The radiance of the sun feeding light into my eyes.
Does he look down and ask the question, how?
How do the plants so effortlessly grow?
They have no concept of tomorrow.

How does a bird so graciously fly?
No concept of, 'that goal is too high.'
How does a dolphin so effortlessly swim?
Each a model of perfection – all three fins.
How does the penguin recognize his mate?
A thousand calls, only one to procreate.
How does the blue whale grow so long?
A human life-age bellowing enchanting songs.
How does a wolf's howl remain crystal clear?
Even when enclosed by mountains front, left and rear.

The answers I do not know
And yet each one has a life which does grow;
Grows independent of human help,
Most likely for the better;
They need no wealth.

All of us intertwined by invisible lines,
A recipe of creation for us to understand later.
Whilst we are in this moment let us seek peace.
The beauty and diversity of life,

The Answers I Do Not Know

A gift from our Creator.

It Lifts Me Up to Heights Unseen

A wonder to behold,
That great God of old.
Walking among us.
Graciously here to admonish.

My Lord and my King,
It is to you my heart does sing.
Great tidings of hope,
For the many wonders you will bring.

From the deepest ocean
To the widest river.
All hope rests
With He who delivers.

I am His and He is divine.
One body and one Head.
A future meeting,
He will judge the dead.

Eternally thankful
For all that is given.
My Lord and my Savior
Put an end to derision.

Merciful and righteous.

It Lifts Me Up to Heights Unseen

Believers will be saved.
A lasting indictment,
Handed to the depraved.

Patience and prudence,
Both wise traits.
Even King Solomon's measure,
No comparison to He who creates.

Time is His tool,
Life is His craft.
To comprehend the chosen One,
No human can grasp that.

Generations come.
Generations go.
The depth of His love,
One day soon all will know.

An ascension like no other.
Through Him we are all brothers.
Greet the gift of grace.
We will lay eyes upon His face.

We bend a knee.
We bow the head.
Humbled in His temple,
We receive the bread.

A gateway to a life of harmony.

His redeeming death instils in me,
A feeling of awe,
A love so pure.

It lifts me up to heights unseen.
Granted eternal status far above any human queen.
Loftier than the highest tower.
May we remain faithful
And escape that final hour.

Giver of Imperishable Treasure

Wise beyond all measure.
Giver of imperishable treasure.
His domain a place for the faithful to attain.
Humility will forever allow us to remain.

Lift up your hearts.
Soon we will depart.
Not a chance thing you see,
For the Holy Spirit to rest within thee.

A gift from God,
Manifest through the Son.
A valiant cause for song,
To unconditionally love everyone.

The conception at Pentecost.
A bid to save all who are lost.
2000 years have passed.
His promise will be made true at last.

With earnest prayer
And selfless deeds.
A meeting in the air,
I implore you to take heed.

He is the One.

He is our Savior.
We will sing His song.
We will mind our behavior.

A fateful epoch.
We have won the lottery,
Being born at the end of humanity's clock.
"Come, follow me."
Empowering words from the Prince of Peace.

Trust in the Lord.
Accept the eternal reward.
We are bond-servants of Christ.
He willingly paid the price.

His life for the world,
I owe Him my allegiance.
Humanity's herald.
May we take joy in showing our obedience.

Scripture referenced: Luke 18:22

We Will Look into His Eyes

My family I pray for you.
Forever I will remain with you.
We will look into His eyes,
Windows to the soul most wise.
Original origin is unknown.
Undoubtedly magnificent to behold.
Master from time long ago.
Maker of all that is unfathomably old.

This path of faith down we go.
Forever destined for our souls to grow.
May we all remember in light of impending events;
That fate defining and soul gratifying covenant,
The one because of which we ought to repent.

God's binding promise,
Spoken to the righteous One, without blemish most honest.
Made known still unknown knowledge,
"Never again shall the water become a flood to destroy all flesh."
A source of hope lest we forget,
The destiny of man not over yet.

Beyond the edges of space,
Into the depths filled with hate.
A timeless entity.
More than gracious to me.

I owe Him my allegiance without measure.
Will you join me in sharing His treasure?

Feel it, believe it,
We need no longer dream it.
We will see His face,
Greeted with a warm embrace.
From the beginning of time,
It is our soul's destiny to forever shine.

The feeling of joy is overwhelming me.
His love has been cast upon me.
His enchanting beauty words cannot describe.
I will end it now with a tear of joy in my eye.

Scripture referenced: Genesis 9:15

Never Again Subject to Sin

He is the King.
To have faith is not going out on a limb.
We will soon be changed forever;
Never again subject to sin.
The game of soul saving we will win.

Turn from derision.
Cleansed in His blood and blessed with clear vision.
Our God and our King;
There is no sin within Him.
Healing and teaching
Myriad upon myriad of humble children.

1000 years to us, only one day to Him.
Bodies patiently sleeping will be raised first on the last day.
From Galilee to Gethsemane it was only He who's head
did not lay.

Strength and power beyond our comprehension.
We will see Him soon at the promised ascension.
My brothers and sisters hold your head up high.
We will be raptured and dwell above the sky.

Many unfortunate souls subject to promulgated fear.
Luke 21:28 "But when these things begin to take place,
Straighten up and lift up your heads,
Because your redemption is drawing near."

The time is at hand.
Join me in taking the final stand.
Clothed in the full armor of God,
No evil will steal my salvation above.
Trust in the Rock of Ages.
It was He who inspired the holy pages.

WE ARE ALL GUILTY

The depth of Christ's soul.
A sculptor of hearts.
Don't be ashamed to love one another,
If you do then evil will depart.

Put aside all darkness.
Put aside all deceit.
Our Father does love us.
Our Savior gives hope to the meek.

We are all guilty,
I'm no exception.
We abuse Christ's love.
We give Him rejection.

The world is not easy.
The world is not fair.
Oh how we've sinned;
Not worthy of His care.

A pain in my heart.
A thorn in my side.
Eternal separation from my Father,
The thought makes me cry.

He will not force us.
His love will convict.

Nevertheless His perfect righteousness,
Sends unrepentant hearts down into the abyss.

I Know the Wait Is Worth It

Up from the depths filled with hate.
All space and time He did create
Our Lord Jesus does admonish.
His flesh bled to fulfil our Father's promise.

Kindness and care He does overflow.
Patience and love set free from what's below.
Encourage the fainthearted.
Christ's generosity for all mankind to know.

A love so strong.
A story so true.
Myriads of angels,
Making supplication for you.

Death is not the end,
This is our beginning.
Maintain faith, hope and love.
It is we who are winning.

Who else is able to endure?
Endure rejection at the majority of doors.
His heart never rejects.
His love never fades.
No human can compare
– He is the Ancient of Days.

Our Lord, He is the One,
Upon His return death shall be overcome.
Our God is perfect.
Amidst all pain and suffering,
I know the wait is worth it.

Thank You Lord for Changing My Heart

One life with each other.
Many sisters, many brothers.
One Father above all.
One Father who loves all.

An extended hand to all He gives.
One life offered to all who live.
He lived and died by the Father's will;
For me and you He overcame,
By dying on that hill.

A word so flippantly used,
Love – forever promised to me and you.
To lay down one's life for a friend.
Our King will rule beyond this world's end.

A most treasured breastplate of faith and love;
Adorned with a helmet of salvation.
Battle array to bring us closer to our Savior;
The One and only – "He will rule all nations."

Thank you Lord for changing my heart.
I know one day You will let us depart;
Let us depart from the face of this earth.
My God and my Savior – You know our true worth.

A worth that surpasses any earthly thing,
It is your worth, my God, that makes my heart sing.
There is only so much a sentence can say;
May I rest in Your love – You will return one day.

Scripture referenced: Revelation 19:15

ACCEPT HIS LOVE AND SACRIFICE

You call Me Father.
I am love.
You call Me God.
I watch from up above.

You call upon My Son,
He hears from heaven above.
You call upon My Son,
But then neglect His unending love.

You'll seek My face and find Me.
I was waiting all along.
You'll find your voice in due time
And then you'll know My glory.

I am the Son from heaven above.
You know Me child, embrace My love.
The world knows Me but yet denies.
Mankind's emancipator.
"He will wipe away every tear from their eyes."

The earth is My footstool.
The truth the enemy misconstrues.
Forsake all evil and fleeting gain.
Accept My love and sacrifice,
Then forever you will remain.

Scripture referenced: Revelation 21:4

FAITH, HOPE AND LOVE

Life travels slow.
The years move fast.
The key to the future,
Embedded in our past.

Fighting and feuding all over the world.
Dreaming and hoping like boys and girls.
Bring your hope back once again.
The King will come,
He will descend.

Faith, hope and love.
May our name be written in His book.
The Lamb's book of life;
Entry free, no monetary price.

A changing of the heart.
A renewing of the mind.
Reverence and awe for our Maker
– He is the universal Creator.

From heaven's end to the depths below.
The magnitude of His might and wonder,
One day we will know.
Are you ready to go?

Love Your Neighbour as Yourself

The beauty of a plant.
Our eternal chant.
The lies and wickedness of evil;
In time He shall supplant.

A meandering road down we go.
First to last, all will know.
An apostasy from hate and greed.
Reliance on Christ,
Not a man-made creed.

Evil people with godly appearance,
Godly people with evil appearance.
Who are we to judge?
The Father is always listening.

A gracious gift of faith and love.
To love one another that is enough.
A task so simple and yet so hard,
Made possible through love for Yeshua.

What is my goal?
What is my purpose?
I follow the commandments.
Am I not yet worth it?

No I am not and neither are we.
None doth enter except by He.
What must I do to please the Lord?
"Love your neighbour as yourself."
We can do no more.

Scripture referenced: Mark 12:31

Through Toils and Terrors

He brought me up out of the pit of destruction.
Through toils and terrors snatched from obstruction.
Lift up your heart to the Ancient of Days
Turn your back on corruption
And embrace the change.

"I waited intently for the Lord."
Worth it for the applause.
Sin will rule no more.

Endless temptation;
Plenty of frustration.
For the glory of the life to come,
I am longingly waiting.

"How blessed is the man who has made the Lord his trust."
Put on the breastplate of righteousness.
Faith is a must.

Wave after wave of useless, wretched, fleshly lust.
Hold steadfast in the Lord,
You will gain His trust.

"I have spoken of your faithfulness and your salvation."
I pray each day Your glory is revealed to every nation.
Sunk down low, dragged into a cycle of despair.
To lay eyes on Your person again,

I belong there.

"For evils beyond number have surrounded me;"
Lifeless, empty, they seek to destroy Your family.
Don't let them my Lord.
Display Your power.

Reveal Your majesty.
At your name they flee.
The chosen King,
Jesus Christ is He.

"Be pleased, O Lord, to deliver me;
Make haste, O Lord, to help me."
Adopted children yet unworthy.
Don't hide Your face my Lord,
It's time to uproot the enemy.

Scripture referenced: Psalm 40:1,4,10,12,13

Find Your Gift and It Will Pay

Down but not defeated.
Your heart will keep on beating.
A most assured source of hope,
In time we will all meet Him.

The granted Savior.
The bravest sailor;
Over choppy waters and stormy seas.
I'll make it home one day,
Safe in the bosom of He.

The mighty man.
The Father's plan.
His Holy Spirit gifted,
We're taking back the land.

It starts with one,
Trump is he.
The modern day Cyrus,
Anointed by God to usher in peace.

You have a gift,
I do too;
It may just be discovered
At the age of sixty two.

Christ was not poor,
He had no guarantor.
At His birth given gifts,
More than fit for a Lord.

Money is a tool.
Your gift should be your craft.
Still not found it yet?
Simply bow your head and ask.

Self-righteous poverty,
It profits no one, certainly not He.
Find your gift and it will pay.
Always remember the needs of the poor,
What the Lord gives He can take away.
Scripture referenced: Job 1:21

He Left His Kingly Estate

Christ is risen.
Christ has ascended.
How blessed is the man,
Whom by Christ is not offended.

Through the cosmos.
Under the ocean.
I watch and wait for Him,
Heaven's door to open.

Blessed from birth,
His wisdom widely known.
His blood's worth;
The believer's ticket home.

He left His kingly estate.
For us He changed His fate.
The Prince to an otherwordly kingdom
Forever we will sing to Him

Not a forced declaration of service.
Not an imposed upon way of worship.

Freely we entrust our soul to He.
Willingly He laid down His life for we.
So often flippantly remarked
– The only reason we will depart.

We Are Claiming Back the Darkness

The winds of change;
A world-view rearranged.
A great gift of God,
To never be the same.

A solemn sunset.
On the rise again – the power of the West.
This is no earthly kingdom.
We will forever sing to Him.

Unseen forces.
Unknown ends;
Only for those whom on Christ do not depend.

This kingdom age;
The dark shall fade.
"I am fearfully and wonderfully made."

"Joint heirs with Christ."
He has snatched us from the night.
No power greater than God's,
There's no match for His insurmountable might.

We have the power.
We have the authority.
Christ stripped the devil;

He now has the keys.

We are God's children,
He is the Father.
"Your kingdom come,
Your will be done."
We are claiming back the darkness.

Scripture referenced: Psalm 139:14, Romans 8:17, Matthew 6:10

The Earth Needs Healing

The skyline soars.
The clouds go boom;
A sight so frightening.
The darkness ends soon.

The mountains erupt.
The rains pour down.
All creation groans,
Until the Lord touches down.

The earth needs healing.
We've heard enough screaming.
To take up our spiritual weapons,
The Lord of all has beckoned.

"Faith as small as a mustard seed."
You are blessed;
These final generations
Consummate their family tree.

"Those destined for captivity,
to captivity they go."
Hold your head up high,
Into the heavenly congregation we go.

Bind the enemies power.
Now is the chosen hour.

Decree and declare,
To the enemy your words will be sour.

Heavenly Father I am your child,
May these words ring true.
I draw powerful angels to me,
Those that swear allegiance to You.

In the name of the Lord Jesus
I give them the authority and power to;
To protect all Your bond-servants,
Especially when they proclaim the truth.

Now is our time.
Pour out Your grace and let us shine.
Bind the unseen enemies,
Cast them into the depths beneath.
Don't hide Your face from us Lord.
I declare Your angels must protect the meek.

Scripture referenced: Matthew 17:20, Revelation 13:10

The Sovereign Soul-Saver

The sovereign soul-saver.
The impartial adjudicator.
Birthed from long ago,
The one and only emancipator.

The sovereign soul-saver.
Earth's foundations lift up their voice to Him.
The miracle maker.
Lift up your heart and sing.
Attune your heart and mind;
"Perfect love casts out fear."
Pay attention to the poor,
Our gracious God is always near.

A heavy price to pay,
Saying no to the world each day.
Not no to her indwelt people,
Just no to the way of sheeple.

Each a gift to call their own,
Each a ticket, a way back home.
Our Father knows and cares,
Who else would count each and every hair?

He gave His only begotten Son,
The man called Jesus Christ.
His heart longs for you to seek Him,
He is the Lord of Light.

Take Control of Your Vessel

I need to get a grip
Or the righteous feast I'll miss.
Useless flesh,
My soul says, 'is this it?'

You don't need this,
You don't want this,
You won't miss it one bit.
Remember, heaven's host says 'stop it!'
A slime covered worm,
An unjust way to earn.
Both a rose amongst thorns,
Compared to your deeds that will burn.

Get a grip,
Rise above it.
Tap into the power that you understand.
Use heaven's forces
To occupy each and every land.

"A blind man cannot guide a blind man, can he?
Will they not both fall into a pit?"
You have both seen and heard,
Now for the love of God – stop it.

Not an empty wish or a dream without foundation.
Not an empty poem seeking man's glory and adoration.

A heartfelt poem with sincere and simple meaning,
Take control of your vessel,
You will soon meet Him.

My latter end,
Heavenward I shall ascend.
Better than my beginning,
I hear the angels singing.

Scripture referenced: Luke 6:39

He Is Your Maker

On my last legs.
My soul will not forget;
His everlasting love.
Grace poured out from up above.

The King of kings,
It is to Him my heart sings.
Down and out,
The enemy encompasses roundabout.
The archangel will give the final shout.

"I will prepare for thee,
A table in the presence of thy enemies."
'Have no fear in your heart,
I will rain upon the earth
A barrage of fiery darts.'

'You will be mocked.
You will be scoffed.
Hold your head up high.
I have only one flock'.

To do the will of our Father,
There is nothing greater.
His love Is unbreakable,
He is your Maker.

Our God Is the King

Our God is the King.
His army will win.
Included in it me and you.
No fear of pain.
No fear of damage;
Protected by Christ through our marriage.

The plains of Esdraelon
Is where we will do battle.
Satan and his minions,
They will be as butchered cattle.

Our God is the King.
His army will win.
Even satan knows this
So cling to the King.

The land soaked in blood,
Not of those blessed from above.
The elect, the chosen, the redeemed.
Hold each other in high esteem.

Created for an eternal purpose.
The Lord Jesus Christ says,
'You are worth it.'

A purpose of love.

A purpose of worship.
A little while longer,
We will be in heaven above.

Scripture referenced: Revelation 14:19-20

An Inbuilt Persistence

An inbuilt persistence.
A longing for more.
When this life is over,
Will you get to heaven's door?

An inbuilt persistence.
A longing for more.
The greatest trick played on man,
To think your ancestors are no more.

Your ancestors and alive,
Some of them are well.
I humbly tell you,
Many are suffering in hell.

Your ancestors are alive,
Some of them are well;
They would want me to tell you,
Don't end up in hell.

Hell is the home of satan,
The adversary from of old;
He prowls around like a lion,
Seeking to destroy your soul.

What is it that destroys your soul?
What is it that makes your bones grow old?

Judgment and division.
Denial of God-given precision.

Many forms of life,
Yet only one can look to the stars at night;
Look to the stars and wonder,
Is there life out there?
We still ponder.

Billions spent searching the stars;
Better spent healing the human heart.
Not healing it with material goods,
But spreading the love of our Father above.

God the Father created us all,
His Son Jesus sent to guide us back home.
This life is not all that there is.
Immortality is Jesus Christ's to give;
Put your hope in Him and live.

IN THIS FESTIVE SEASON

There is no Christmas without Christ.
He is the heir to heaven's throne.
It is He who passed through darkness to light.

We say merry Christmas.
We all have a wish list.
Often we say, 'oh, how I'll miss this.'

There's nothing we'll miss.
There's no Christmas gift,
That can even come close,
To being about the Father's business.

The Lord is alive.
Open your eyes.
The Rock of Ages.
A love contagious.
God the Creator,
He's the One that made us.

Christmas is a time of giving;
A momentary pause from division.
It is a time to be grateful.
Christ doesn't want our lives to be wasteful.

How long do you have on this earth?
"70 years or if due to strength 80."

It could take that long to know your worth.

I'm sharing the Good News with you today.
The Lord Jesus Christ has already paved the way.

The first step to salvation
– Admit you're a sinner.
Step number two
– Accept that Jesus is the winner.

The only One to conquer death and the grave.
The only One in the underworld for three days.

Jesus Christ changed my life.
He is the overcomer of night.
In this festive season,
This time of giving;
I humbly tell you we will all meet Him.

Scripture referenced: Psalm 90:10

The Joy of the Lord Is Your Strength

"The joy of the Lord is your strength."
Placing faith in man-made vaccines,
God did not invent.
The human body made perfect by our Father.
'Let's push the body further and further.'
The mantra of Big Pharma.

'Three weeks to stop the spread.'
Two years later...
How many other false hopes have been said?

They don't care about you.
They don't care about me.
They do care about propping up
Their magic money tree.

'One vaccine is good.'
'Two vaccines are great.'
Now you'll need them all the time;
It's the only way to be safe.

We enter the world with nothing
And that's exactly how we'll leave.
The only thing that matters,
When we come face to face with Jesus Christ,
Will He reject us or will He be pleased?

FOR HE HIMSELF IS OUR PEACE

"For He Himself is our peace."
With Jesus Christ we'll feast.
The Rock of Ages.
The Prince of Peace.
In time all will meet.
"By His wounds we are healed."
He said remember Me during their final meal.
He knew all that was to come
And yet He was not overcome.

"Father, the hour has come, glorify Your Son…"
The weight of the world on His shoulders.
Through His resurrection satan was overcome.

Scripture referenced: Ephesians 2:14, 1 Peter 2:24, John 17:1

As in the Days of Noah

A quiet moment.
A peaceful day.
Thanks to Jesus Christ,
We'll live beyond the end of days.

Good is called evil and evil is called good.
God's righteous anger kindled up above.

"As in the days of Noah."
So it will be at the end.
Many will not believe
Until Jesus Christ descends.

Jesus Christ is coming back,
Is your heart ready for that?
If He were to descend,
On whom would you depend?

People like Bill Gates?
Or God who effortlessly creates.
Where would your hope be?
If not God then all is vanity.

A whole generation.
A spiritual degradation.
No comprehension of a physical
To spiritual transcendental ascension.

A whole generation hostile toward God.
How we've been mistaken.

God is the source of life.
Now is the time to get right.
Get right with Jesus Christ.
Who knows? Tonight may be your final night.

Scripture referenced: Isaiah 50:20, Matthew 24:37

Satan Will Suffer the Last Defeat

The Lord is my peace.
Satan will suffer the last defeat;
Thrown into the "lake of fire,"
All of his followers he'll meet.

Sounds of thunder and peals of lightning.
The sight of God, oh so frightening.
He watches, He waits.
His Son's death,
Who chooses to contemplate?

Jesus Christ is His name.
He bore all our shame.
Seek His existence,
You'll be forever saved.

Scripture referenced: Revelation 20:10

Seek Peace and Pursue It

"The Lord is a strong fortress."
The host of heaven will applaud us.

When our race is run and we've passed the test,
Our heavenly Father will call us,
He'll say, 'enter into My rest.'

Turn from wordly obsessions.
Let Jesus' life be the lesson.

"Seek peace and pursue It."
To offer immortality,
Only Jesus Christ can do it.

Not a vain ambition
Of a self-centered man.
Faith like a child.
This is the Creator's plan.

Supernatural beings.
Made to be fulfilled.
Supernatural beings.
It is the Father's will.

Heaven is our home.
Heaven is a place.
To live and die as one of us,

Jesus took our place.

Scripture referenced: Psalm 18:2, Hebrews 4:3, Psalm 34:14, 1 Peter 3:11

In a World of War and Greed

In a world of war and greed,
It's Jesus Christ we need.
The sovereign soul-saver.
Paid mankind the biggest favor.

"Wars and rumors of wars…
But that is not yet the end."
Conflict, judgment and hatred…
If only of Jesus Christ we'd depend.

A glimpse into the future.
No more man-made computers.
"The city has no need of the sun."
Through Jesus Christ darkness is overcome.

Scripture referenced: Matthew 24:6, Revelation 21:23

King of Kings

King of kings and
Lord of salvation.
Beyond all this conflict,
He will rule all nations.

King of kings and
Lord of salvation.
One day the sun will rise
And the believers will have been taken.

A stairway to heaven,
There's an open door.
Thanks to the Lord Jesus Christ,
Death will be no more.

KINGS, PRIESTS AND PROPHETS

Kings, priests and prophets.
Jesus is always honest.
We're to rule and reign with Christ.
We're not to give in to fright.

"God is our refuge and strength,
A very present help in trouble."
God is over every conflict,
Always left standing above the rubble.

Jesus Christ is Lord of all the earth.
Jesus Christ knows our true worth.
Pray for protection of believers in Ukraine.
Pray God will make earth's leaders
Righteous once again.

Scripture referenced: Psalm 46:1

The Earth Is His Footstool

"The earth is My footstool."
The earth is His creation.
At the end of all things,
He will pour out revelation.

God's ways are not our ways.
Nothing about Him is natural.
Millions read the bible.
Many less acknowledge,
There's nothing more supernatural.

Scripture referenced: Isaiah 66:1

What Has Been Before

"That which has been
Is that which will be again."
Good vs evil.
A cycle that will finally end.

God the Father,
Seated in the heavens.
Wicked rulers make their plans.
No wiser than a child of eleven.

"I will pour out My Spirit on all flesh."
The evidence of Christ's existence,
Will take a monumental effort to reject.

Scripture referenced: Ecclesiastes 1:9 (AMP), Joel 2:28

Joe Biden Will Fall

Joe Biden will fall,
Donald Trump will be re-elected;
The Supreme Court will be involved,
The Western media will be corrected.

Jesus Will See Us Through

It's all for You.
I do it all for You.
Jesus will see us through.
Overwhelming proof.

Satan makes it easier to sin.
God makes it easier to discover Him.
God's will is insurmountable.
To deny His existence is fanciful.

Are we reading what we believe
Or believing what we read?

Jesus said Himself,
"For nothing will be impossible with God."
A woman of 90,
Sarah multiplied mankind's family tree.

A testament to her faith.
For many years she had to wait;
Wait for the birth of Isaac,
Can you believe a miracle such as this?

Scripture referenced: Luke 1:37

God Is the Referee

God is the referee.
Life is the game;
The rules that have seen set
Cannot be changed.

Remember who you are
And what you were sent to do.
Breathe it all in,
Your soul will thank you.

You came to discover Christ,
So you could have eternal life.
Life in heaven eternal gain.
Death in hell eternal pain.

CHILDREN OF LIGHT

Children of light.
Made by the "Father of lights."
His overwhelming desire,
We accept His Son and eternal life.

"The Father of spirits."
"The Ancient of Days."
To love Jesus He wills it,
A state attained if we change our ways.

He loves us dearly.
No number of prayers could make Him weary.
Jesus is the only way to heaven
– There'll be no 'nearly.'

Scripture referenced: James 1:17, Hebrews 12:9, Daniel 7:9

What You Enter Into

Saved us with His blood.
Jesus Christ the Lord above,
Holy, humble and gracious.
It was His love that saved us.

What you enter into
Will enter into you.
The soul is a sponge,
It remembers all you do.

"Seek first His kingdom and righteousness…"
Not that which burdens us.
"And all these things will be added to you."
Don't worry about what
The godless news tells you to do.

Scripture referenced: Matthew 6:33

Everything Changes Through Jesus

We were dead in our trespasses
In which we formerly walked.
Everything changes through Jesus.
He sought the Father, They talked.

Sent on a mission from heaven.
Anointed wisdom at the age of eleven.
"In Him we have the redemption through His blood...
According to the riches of His grace,
Which He lavished on us."
Scripture referenced: Ephesians 1:7-8

No Longer in Bondage

No longer in bondage.
You made me stronger.
No longer in bondage.
You are our warrior.

"Why do you boast in evil, O mighty man?"
Have you not heard?
There is only God's plan.

"The loving-kindness of God
Endures all day long."
Thanks to Jesus Christ,
His saints will join in heaven's song.

Scripture referenced: Psalm 52:1

Lord, Send Your Fire

Fear, it's passing.
His love, it's everlasting.
Lord, send Your fire.
Lord, take the church higher.

"The Spirit of truth who proceeds from the Father."
The Helper in times of need.
To reveal all things from the Father,
On our behalf the Holy Spirit pleads.

Time to awake from our slumber.
God's got satan's number.
Every plan satan ever made...
Jesus will still have His way.

Scripture referenced: John 15:26

I Am with You Always

"I am with you always."
His love exhorts we change.

No greater commandment than to love God;
Made possible by keeping our
Mind set on things above.

Jesus laid down His life for His friends;
More importantly,
For those who brought about His end.

An end to His time as a man.
On the third day He rose
Completing the Father's plan.

Scripture referenced: Matthew 28:20

A Father of the Fatherless

"A father of the fatherless
And a judge for the widows."
What does tomorrow hold?
Only God can know.
He controls time.
He made space.
Hope of what's to come,
Gifted to us through grace.

"Declaring the end from the beginning."
The enemy thinks they're winning.
God stopped the sun for a whole day.
Evil will not rule in the coming days.

Scripture referenced: Psalm 68:5, Isaiah 46:10, Joshua 10:13

For He Is Coming

"For He is coming to judge the earth."
"Coming on the clouds of the sky."
A sound that has not yet been heard.

"Then the trees of the forest will sing for joy."
And all the earth will have lasting peace.
The armies of heaven,
God will no longer need to deploy.

Scripture referenced: 1 Chronicles 16:33, Matthew 24:30

The Only Way to Be Victorious

There will be a war in the heavens,
It's already begun.
The only way to be victorious,
Is to stay close to the Son.

The Son of Man.
The Prince of Peace.
The only King
Who never tasted defeat.

The Son of Man.
It was the Father's divine plan.
He died for every man and woman,
To avoid hell if they can.

HE CREATED THE STARS

He created the stars.
He created the heavens.
To really know the Lord,
Takes curiosity of a child that's eleven.

He created the snow.
He created the rain.
Put your hope in Jesus,
You'll be forever changed.

The plants grow through all the seasons.
Like the believer they long to see Him.
Don't lose heart,
Jesus always wins.

If God Let Everyone Go to Heaven

If God let everyone go to heaven,
It would be no different to the earth.
Arguments, death, and hate.
Satan doesn't want you to know your worth.

Satan doesn't want your destiny to be fulfilled,
But Jesus Christ does.
He wants you to seek Him,
With your free will.

Free will does exist.
Free will is a force.
Yuval Noah Harari,
A prophet akin to Santa Clause.

Observe How the Trees Grow

Come rain or snow,
Observe how the trees grow,
To us it may seem slow.
There is a lot we don't know.

Their shoots ascend upward
Glorifying the Creator;
Trying to get closer to the sun.
A small representation of our Maker.

The sun gives light,
It overpowers the night.
A small representation of our Maker.
In the end it's Him that is the Creator.

But Take Courage

Father, I bring all my problems and troubles to you;
I know You'll sort them out.
You always do.

"I will never leave you nor forsake you."
Be warned, the world will hate you;
Hate you because you're different,
Even so, you'll bring souls into the Kingdom.

"In the world you have tribulation."
Be faithful, He'll give you revelation.
"But take courage; I have overcome the world."
In all things, be like little boys and girls.

Scripture referenced: Hebrews 13:5, John 16:33

HE CREATED US

"The law of the Lord is perfect,
Restoring the soul."
He created us.
He knows what we need to be made whole.

"The testimony of the Lord is sure,
Making wise the simple."
There's no aging in heaven,
Not a single wrinkle.

"The fear of the Lord is clean,
Enduring forever,
The judgments of the Lord are true,
They are righteous altogether."
No amount of gold
Can compare to heaven's treasure.
Scripture referenced: Psalm 19:7, Psalm 19:9

How Blessed Is the Man

"How blessed in the man who
Has made the Lord His trust."
He stores up treasure in heaven,
Where it will never rust.

"And has not turned to the proud."
He ignores the ways of the world.
Godless leaders, he turns the other way,
As they spew lies each and every day.

"Nor to those who lapse into falsehood."
Those with no regard for the things above.
Jesus is "the way, the truth and the life."
Only with His love can we overcome strife.
Scripture referenced: Psalm 40:4, John 14:6

All Can Be Set Free

You left the 99 to find me
"Lord I am Your servant."
Only You can deliver me.

Strong and tall like an Oak tree.
Thanks to Jesus Christ,
All can be set free.

"Wars and rumors of wars."
All creation cries,
'Please no more.'

The saved will form a great assembly.
Thanks to Jesus Christ,
War will be nothing but a distant memory.

Scripture referenced: Psalm 116:16, Matthew 24:6

The Lord Waits

Salvation is free but there's a price once you accept it.
The Lord waits, He gazes down.
He died for every human,
So they could know their purpose now.

A king between Christ and man was never needed.
To be given a human ruler;
With God the Jews pleaded.

Saul was the first,
How did that turn out?
The courage of king David,
His lineage the chosen way out.

Haman Paid the King

"That which has been
Is that which will be again."
These are days of renewal,
Just like the days of Haman.

Haman paid the king
And he thought his plan would win.
He built the gallows for an execution,
He never thought it would be for him.

Satan's people planned to take our freedom,
Shortly they will meet Him.
Jesus has plans for joy and justice.
His body prepared for a time such as this.

Scripture referenced: Ecclesiastes 1:9

HIS ARMS WIDE OPEN

God is faithful.
He keeps our seat at His table.
It's our actions not His,
That cause us to reminisce.

His arms wide open
After we've drank satan's potion.
The prodigal son was always welcome.
The oppressed will make it to heaven.

"Where there is no guidance the people fall."
Seek Jesus and live forevermore.
"But in abundance of counselors there is victory."
The best counselor is the Prince of Peace.

Scripture referenced: Proverbs 11:14

OUR FATHER AND ADONAI

Jesus Christ is the source of life,
In this life and in the afterlife.
Jesus said,
"I am the resurrection and the life…"
The only lasting source of peace,
In this world filled with strife.

Turn to Him and be set free.
Turn to Him and live a life of victory.

"Whoever believes in Me will live even if he dies."
The world and all it contains was not
Created by a simple man in the sky.
It was created by the Great God of old.
He is our Father and Adonai.

Scripture referenced: John 11:25

My Father's Business

Jesus is coming back,
No question about that.
Open your heart to that
Embrace it when people laugh.

From a young boy
"Jesus was strong in spirit,
Filled with wisdom and grace."
God the Father willed it.

"Did you not know?
I had to be about My Father's business."
His mother Mary loved Him
But couldn't comprehend this.
His Father is God the Creator.
His business to reveal God's nature.

Scripture referenced: Luke 2:40 (AMP), Luke 2:49 (KJV)

Pharaoh Was Just a Man

"The Lord is slow to anger."
Not quick to lose His temper.
"Zeal for your house will consume Me."
Saved His people from Pharaoh surely.

"That which has been
Is that which will be again."
Satan's plans cast asunder.
Jesus is the God of thunder.

The Rock of Ages.
The Lord of Hosts.
Pharaoh was just a man,
In his own strength did he boast.

Many pharaohs around today,
Protecting their dam of truth.
Soon it will be broken,
God's power will be on display.

Scripture referenced: Numbers 14:18, Nahum 1:3, John 2:17, Ecclesiastes 1:9

Every Need Provided For

A mystery revealed to me,
Through Jesus we are given victory.
Victory over death and hell.
Hope in Jesus, all will be well.

The best of times and the worst of times,
Both are on the way.
Every need provided for,
To those that seek God's ways.

"He sends rain on the just
And on the unjust."
To make sense of coming global changes,
Faith in Christ is a must.

Scripture referenced: Matthew 5:45 (ESV)

THE WORLD IS BEING SHAKEN

Take dominion through love.
Grace poured out from up above.
We are to rule and reign with Christ,
Not to give in to fright.

The world is being shaken.
God is giving revelation.
A time of longing souls.
A new church walking bold.

Old ways made obsolete;
Spiritually dead suffer defeat.
The preacher and the prophet will stand.
Jesus Christ will be proclaimed across the land.

A Difficult Paradox

Christ is the vine.
Mankind made divine.
An open invitation,
To live beyond all time.

The universe is governed by good.
Our deeds are recorded from above.

A difficult paradox;
To be humble as a child,
To befriend almighty God.

Be humbled like a child,
It may take a little while.
Be assured when death comes,
You'll greet it with a smile.

This Is the Essence of True Love

We take it upon ourselves
To judge the weight of another's sin;
A mindset that gets us nowhere,
We need to put it in the bin.

Satanists are made in God's image too.
Without Jesus all will burn in hell.
They've been lied to by demons,
They need prayers of salvation as well.

Jesus prayed for those who killed Him.
This is the essence of true love.
Without it we're no use
To our heavenly Father above.

Ascending the Eternal Staircase

Ascending the eternal staircase.
I'll someday see the Father's face.
All the angels in rapturous applause;
Another child made it back home.

"On earth as it is in heaven."
Family, nature and faith,
It was God that did create.

Many forms of life and only one can
Look to the stars at night,
Look to the stars and wonder.
On the last day God will bring the thunder.

Scripture referenced: Matthew 6:10

Don't Give Up

"The peace of God,
which surpasses all understanding."
One day all will stand before Him.
Some to everlasting gain.
Some to everlasting pain.

The earth created for us all,
Even the ones who fall.
"God is love."
He looks down from above.

Life gets hard,
Don't give up.
Jesus wants you to know,
You've always been loved.

Scripture referenced: Philippians 4:7 (ESV), 1 John 4:8

Pass Through Life's Trials

"For a time such as this."
Pass through life's trials,
On the other side is bliss.
"The peace of God,
which surpasses all understanding."
In heaven there's always those that sing.
Jesus is the King,
Follow Him and always win.

The world looks lawless.
The world looks mean.
When God moves His hand,
He'll reveal all that's unseen.

Scripture referenced: Esther 4:14, Philippians 4:7 (ESV)

All the Mysteries of God to Reveal

A great God and Adonai.
He reigns from far above the sky.
All the mysteries of God to reveal.
We have to ask Him, why?

2000 years ago upon a cross.
2000 years later the world has not forgot.
Satan is the father of lies,
He convinces people there's no God on high.

More faith to believe we came from nothing;
Than to believe God made us for His pleasure
And so that we would sing.

Sing of His mighty works.
Sing of His awesome power.
To escape death and hell,
Look to Jesus in your darkest hour.

Glory to God

Glory to God.
His ways are righteous.
Will we humble ourselves?
Will we become one of His?

Tomorrow's not promised but eternity is.
Will you humble yourself?
Will you become one of His?

A love the world can't offer.
A hope no bribe can give.
Humble oneself like a child.
Believe in Jesus and live.

THE FULLNESS THEREOF

"The earth is the Lord's
And the fullness thereof."
The earth is the Lord's.
Will you accept His love?

A love that's unending.
His return impending.
Beyond the troubles of life,
We will forever worship Him.

It takes a long time
To get to know God.
It takes a long time,
We came from above.

The soul and the spirit,
They will live forever.
To walk with Jesus,
There's nothing better.

Scripture referenced: 1 Corinthians 10:26 (ESV)

THE HOUR IS HERE

The hour is here.
The hour is now.
How will you be remembered in eternity?
Will you take the vow?

A vow to accept Jesus.
Only He can heal us.
A vow to accept Jesus.
Only He can hear us.
When our heart longs
For peace and meaning,
Will we be humbled?
Will we draw near to Him?

"The earth is the Lord's
And all it contains."
When death comes He won't be heard saying,
'OK, you can try again '

Scripture referenced: 1 Corinthians 10:26

The Prince of Peace

"The Rock of Ages."
"The Prince of Peace."
In time all will meet.

"The KING OF KINGS,
The LORD OF LORDS."
Now He guides my feet.

Jesus Christ is His name.
He bore all our shame.
He gave His life on the cross.
The world never the same.

A peace beyond all understanding.
It's not about us;
It's about Him.

"You keep him in perfect peace,
Who's mind is stayed on You."
One day all will know,
To believe in Jesus is true.

"Wars and rumors of wars,
But that is not yet the end."
You'll store up treasure in heaven,
If on Jesus Christ you'll depend.

He Restores My Soul

"He restores my soul."
Your return has been foretold.
Jesus is your name.
The world never the same.

"Humility comes before honor."
Satan looks for easy fodder.
"Many will see and fear."
A great change is near.

"How blessed is the man who makes
The Lord his trust."
To escape hell fire,
Faith in Jesus is a must.

He died for your sins
And He died for mine.
Thanks to Jesus Christ,
You can live beyond all time.
All time is unending.
Heaven will forever sing;
Not a boring place,
But the home of God,
Filled with unimaginable things.

"70 years or if due to strength 80."
Then what?

There's no reincarnation
As a newborn baby.

You have an eternal soul.
You have an eternal destination.
Thanks to Jesus Christ,
When death comes you'll meet it with expectation.

Scripture referenced: Psalm 23:3, Proverbs 15:33, Psalm 40:4, 90:10

Won't Stop Singing

Jesus has the power,
It's written in the book of Isaiah.
He is earth's King.
He always wins.

"Who announced this rise of Cyrus
Long before it happened?"

"Who declared it long ago."
Jesus is in control.
"Was it not I, the LORD?"
He's always in control.
"Declaring the end and the result from the beginning."
God's army is winning.
Shortly God's children won't stop singing.

Scripture referenced: Isaiah 45:21 (AMP), Isaiah 46:10 (AMP)

A Time to Reap

The perfect life is
Found in Jesus Christ.
He passed from death to life.
It'll all be alright.

"You caused judgment to be heard from heaven;
The earth feared and was quiet."
When God moves His hand,
Who will be able to deny it?

A time to sow
And a time to reap.
The ones who oppressed God's children,
In hell's company they'll keep.

Scripture referenced: Psalm 76:8 (AMP), Ecclesiastes 3:2

GET IN THE WORD

"The LORD is in His holy temple,
The LORD's throne is in heaven."
He looks down from unapproachable light,
He and the seven.

"The seven spirits of God."
An eternal being of infinite power.
The earth shook when He raised Christ from the dead,
Awesome might on display in that final hour.

A final hour Is upon us.
Satan's grip is fleeting.
Get in the word
And pray without ceasing.
Scripture referenced: Psalm 11:4, Revelation 4:5, 5:6

Eternal Source of Bliss

"He Himself took our infirmities
And carried away our diseases."
Of course I'm talking about Jesus.

"Then He got up and rebuked
The winds and the sea,
And it became perfectly calm."
Non compared to the power of He.

"What kind of a man is this,
That even the winds and the sea obey Him?"
His name is Jesus,
The only eternal source of bliss.

"But they put new wine into fresh wineskins,
And both are preserved."
The Pharisees were set in their ways,
Jesus made them unnerved.

"Daughter, your faith has made you well."
Jesus healed all who came to Him.
Upon each miracle He did not dwell.

The Son of God.
He always wins.
He paved the way,
For all manner of things.

"Greater works than these he will do."
Christ said it
– He only speaks truth.

*Scripture referenced: Matthew 8:17,26,27, 9:17,
Mark 5:34, John 14:12*

Sword of the Spirit

"You will be hated by all because of My name."
By His shame the road was paved.
"But it is the one who has endured
To the end who will be saved."

"Therefore do not fear them,
For there is nothing concealed
That will not be revealed."
In heaven all are healed.

"Do not think that I came to bring
Peace on the earth."
Only Jesus knows your true worth.

He came to divide with the
Sword of the Spirit.
God the Father wills it.
"The blind receive sight
And the lame walk."
Jesus did much more than talk.

"The poor have the gospel preached to them."
"You have hidden these things from the wise and intelligent."
No amount of miracles
Would make the proud repent.

"He began to denounce the cities in

Which most of His miracles were done."
They saw the impossible
And still rejected God's Son.

"Come to Me,
All who are weary and heavy laden,
And I will give you rest."
Jesus will put your soul to the test.
Seek Him or be like the rest.

*Scripture referenced: Matthew 10:22,26,34,
Matthew 11:5,25,20,28*

No House Divided

"No house divided against itself will be able to stand."
Jesus proclaimed the good news,
All across the land.

"On the day of judgment
People will have to give an accounting
For every careless or useless word they speak;"
All whilst seated at God's feet.
The men on Nineveh
And the queen of Sheba;
These will bear witness at the judgment.
Jesus couldn't have made it any clearer.

A gracious God and a humble King.
"Who is my mother and who are my brothers?"
But those that do the will of Him.

Scripture referenced: Mark 3:25, Matthew 12:36 (AMP), Matthew 12:48

The Mysteries of God

Some seed falls and withers.
Some falls and grows with vigor.
With signs the Jews had become enchanted.
"To know the mysteries of God
It had not been granted."

"You will hear and keep on hearing,
But never understand."
This is what it's like,
For the proud who always have to be in command.

"The One who sows the good seed is
The Son of Man."
Give your life to Jesus
And you'll be used in God's plan.

I am alive because of Jesus.
I am alive, He has healed us.
"Herod had John arrested."
Because of an oath he had to be beheaded.

"They do not need to go away,
You give them something to eat!"
Jesus always provided abundance,
To those who took no offence when He'd speak.

'He said, "Come!" So Peter got out of the boat,

And walked on the water and came to Jesus.'
To those who believe,
Jesus will always meet us.

Scripture referenced: Matthew 13:11, 13:14 (AMP),
Matthew 13:37, 14:3, 14:16, 14:29

A Simpler Life

A simpler life.
One free from strife.
"A thousand year reign."
They'll be one husband and one wife.

A simpler life.
Far less technology
To keep us up at night.

People will live off the land.
Jesus will be in command.
The glory of the Lord;
Sweat and toil will be no more.

A hundred lines of men.
Two Adams;
One caused us to fall,
The other brought peace forevermore.

Peace to those that would accept His sacrifice.
Peace to those who come out
Of the darkness and into the light.
Made possible by Jesus Christ.

He watches and waits.
Do His children anticipate?
Anticipate His glorious return?
For all the wonders of heaven do they yearn?

GLORY TO JESUS

Glory to Jesus, it's Him that redeems us.
"1000 years to us is but one day to the Lord."
He's been from the beginning to the end.
He saw all that came before.

Stand up and shout.
His angels encamp roundabout.
He's given His faithful children heaven's keys;
We only have to say yes please.

"For the weapons of our warfare are not carnal,
But mighty through God to the pulling down of strongholds."
The world is about to be drastically changed,
By the great God of old.

Scripture referenced: 2 peter 3:8, 2 Corinthians 10:4

All Flesh and Bone

Generation after generation.
The Lord looks down.
He pours out revelation.

All born of a woman.
All flesh and bone.
Only Jesus Christ
Can change a heart of stone.

The angels who chose lust
Fell from the sky;
Forced to watch their children die
As tears fell from their eyes.

God's judgments are binding.
God's judgments are true.
Not long now,
Society will be made new.

"Woe to those who call evil good."
God's righteous judgment
Hurled down from above.

"When the wicked are cut off,
You will see It."
The wicked will be judged,
Jesus will see to it.

The glory of God will be revealed;
Many people will be healed.
Healed in both body and mind.
The mercy of God makes a soul divine.
Scripture referenced: Isaiah 5:20, Psalm 37:34

The Day Will Come

He is a mighty God.
He reigns from above.
The day will come,
When He withdraws His love.

Descending in glory and power.
A fearful sight in that final hour.
His love will be withdrawn.
No place for evil when the new world dawns.

Time while you're still alive.
Time to accept Christ
And allow your soul to thrive.

Your soul longs to meet the Creator.
Open your heart to Jesus;
After all, He is your Maker.

This life is filled with challenges.
This life is filled with obstacles.
The road can be made smooth,
If you apply Jesus' parables.

When all is said and done.
When death comes and your race is run;
Will you look back with content,
Or with aches and pains lament?

Lament that you didn't open your eyes
To Jesus Christ.
The One who reigns from on high
— He is our Adonai.

Lined with Pearls

Thank you my King
For helping us win;
The battle for our souls.
It has been foretold.

Though the body grows old,
Just a blink of an eye to the soul.
Humble yourself before Christ.
Become friends with the great God of old.

A great God and friend.
He's with us to the end.
The end of this current world.
His city walls are lined with pearls.

The Ground Shakes

"He turned the sea into dry land,
They passed through the river on foot."
The mighty army of pharaoh,
In a moment they stopped and shook.

"Jesus Christ is the same yesterday and today and forever."
Without Christ there is no clever.
"The fear of the Lord is the beginning of wisdom."
Revere Him and you will see Him.
A caring Father and a humble friend.
Nursing us like babies,
Encouraging us to make it to the end.

The rising sun.
A waning moon.
The power of God
Will be seen soon.

The ground shakes at His presence.
The sun is frozen in its place.
Corrupt politicians,
It will soon be time to vacate.

The days grow shorter.
His return draws near.
The glory of God revealed.
Many will be frozen in fear.

EVERY DEED RECORDED

"Christ is the vine."
In Him we're made divine.
John fifteen one.
We should listen to the Son.

He overcame death and the grave.
Jesus Christ paved the way;
The way for peace this day.
His love exhorts we change.

The time is ticking,
The clock is counting.
Every deed recorded;
Better than any accountant.

One heaven and one hell.
The blood of Jesus makes our soul well.
Offered as a propitiation
In what manner will you depart life's station?

By faith we don't depend on our eyes;
The only way to attain life's prize.
Commit your way to the Lord
And you'll live in heaven forevermore.

We run our race.
He guides our walk.

Jesus brings peace,
When we hear Him talk.

He left His home
And all that He had known.
He descended so that we could ascend.

Life can be a great mountain;
A safe route to the top,
If on Jesus we'll depend.

Scripture referenced: John 15:1

A Day Is Coming

Observation and reputation.
The Lord keeps waiting.
Will we seek His salvation?

He created us all;
From the biggest to the small.
We will judge the ones who fall;
They'll be seen no more.

A righteous God.
A faithful King.
Accept Jesus as Lord and Savior.
You will forever sing.

Lord open my heart.
Send your fiery darts.
The day will come
When I will depart.

A day is coming
And an hour now is;
Th power of God on display
– The world is His.

A time to reap
The seeds that have been sown;
The wicked to judgment,

The righteous to abundance foretold.

Those who teach and preach,
In God's presence they keep.
Those who pray everyday.
Those who seek the Lord's ways.

"The wealth of the sinner is stored up for the righteous."
The world's never seen anything like this.

Glory to Jesus,
He has redeemed us.
Glory to Jesus,
He died for us.

Satan's systems will crumble.
The earth already rumbles.
Get right with Jesus
Or you'll be left frantic in a concrete jungle.

Scripture referenced: Proverbs 13:22

Rightful Positions

Christ is all we need,
Only He can set us free.
He died upon a tree.
By His blood we are redeemed.

A people of the Word and the Spirit.
Seek revelation from God.
Through relationship with Christ,
We are able to fulfil it.

As the world grows in darkness
The light will shine brighter.
Through hope in His promises,
You'll be made a fighter.

Corruption and collapse,
Not a thing of the past.
Salvation through Jesus,
For eternity it will last.

Rightful positions will be taken.
The wicked found dead.
"I have not seen the righteous forsaken
Or his descendants begging bread."

Scripture referenced: Psalm 37:25

LOVE HAS A FACE

Lift up your heart to God;
His blessings will rain down from above.
He's "the same yesterday and today and forever."
He's with us through all weather.

Moses had a stutter,
John lived in the wilderness.
The only thing that matters,
You know you're one of His.

Times of plenty and times of feasts.
Times of sadness and times of defeat.
Times of wickedness and times of righteousness;
One constant through it all
– Jesus died for us.

Love has a face,
His name is Jesus.
Love has a face,
He's the source of grace.

The Son of Man,
He is God's plan.
Love poured out,
To every woman and man.

Jesus is a place of peace.

In His throne room we'll feast.
A train coming to the earth,
A new sound never heard.

Scripture referenced: Hebrews 13:8

He Is the Only Way

Changes in time;
Many will pay for their crimes.
The Jews will live in "peace and safety,"
Before the wicked are pressed into wine.

Time has quickened;
God is on the move.
"Plans to give you a hope and a future."
Jesus Christ died for you.

Change is never easy;
New norms rarely welcomed.
Jesus shook the earth to its core,
So that bondage would be no more.

In bondage through the finances,
Thankfully God will rescue us.
Become a follower of Christ today.
He is the only way.
Before the earth was He is;
No force greater than this.
A dark and silent void.
God's power satan tried to avoid.

A great chasm
And a burning flame.
Peace in paradise,

Lazarus was forever changed.

The sound of thunder
And a howling wind;
The presence of the Lord,
None can withstand Him.

"The earth is the Lord's
And all it contains."
When He moves His hand
Nothing will stay the same.

Scripture referenced: 1 Thessalonians 5:3, Jeremiah 29:11, Psalm 24:1, Luke 16:19-31

A NEW REALITY LOOMING

His grace abounds,
Just look at the work of His hands.
To put faith in Christ,
The destiny of man.

From winter rain
To vast open plains;
The glory of God,
Nature proclaims to this day.

A field of poppies.
A sky of clouds.
Don't believe what the news tells you,
Turn from the proud.

An intense season of warfare,
Wicked people and lawfare.
It's coming to a close,
God's children will be made whole.

The flowers are blooming.
A new reality looming;
Pharaoh at the foot of the sea,
About to be humbled by He.

Who is he?
The Prince of Peace.

Abide in Christ,
Share in the feast.

The moment of greatest despair
Is when God descends on the air.
For the passing systems of this world,
I do not care.

The world in His hands,
Never had a failed plan.
His dominion is over every land
– Jesus Christ is all around.

The Glorious King

The glorious King,
His army will win.
When all's said and done,
All of heaven will sing.

Will you be among them?
Will you be there?
When you stand before God,
You'll do nothing but stare.

"Prepare your minds for action."
The words of the apostle Peter.
An endless production of fruit,
If to God we'll draw near.

Not fruit of the physical
But fruit of the Spirit.
Not fruit that perishes,
God the Father wills it.

Born again to a living hope,
One without the Pope.
One hope to make it through this life
– His name is Jesus Christ.

"He's the overseer of our souls."
He walks beside us as we grow old.

"He Himself bore our sins in His body on the tree,
So that we may die to sin and live righteously."

This world is broken and in need of healing.
One day all will stand before Him.
His name is Jesus Christ,
He is the giver of life,
He passed through darkness to light,
So that we could have eternal life.

Now is the time to get right;
Become born again,
Step into a new life.

Scripture referenced: 1 Peter 1:13, 1 Peter 2:25, 1 Peter 2:24 (ESV)

THE CROSS OF CHRIST

The cross of Christ
Opened the door to an afterlife.
It was Jesus who paid the price;
He understands what it's like to live a human life.

"Mocked and flogged and crucified."
It is no lie,
Jesus Christ is our Adonai.
He will forever reign on high.

"He is coming on the clouds."
God's army will shout aloud.
In the company of two thieves,
Only one would be redeemed.

"He showed them His hands and His side."
Jesus had been made alive.
The Pharisees mocked and laughed;
They're now burning in hell,
How they regretted that.

Jesus raised Lazarus from the dead.
He fed thousands so they wouldn't go unfed.
"From that day on the Pharisees planned together to kill Him."
Little did they know,
His death would bring about the greatest win.

He conquered death and the grave.
By God's power He was remade,
In the underworld for three days;
The destiny of man forever changed.

Why don't you change the course of your life today?
Open your heart to Jesus Christ,
He is the truth, the life and the way.

Scripture referenced: Matthew 20:19, Revelation 1:7, John 20:20, John 11:53

The Triumphal Entry

"Look, the whole world has gone running after Him!"
How the Pharisees were misled
To do the will of satan.

"Unless a grain of wheat falls into the earth and dies."
It remains a single grain,
It cannot multiply.

The same idea shown in Jesus' life,
He had to die to make all things right.
Through His death as a sinless man
It brought to completion the Father's plan.

The triumphal entry,
The palm branches were plenty;
"Blessed is the one who comes in the name of the Lord."
Satan's power over the world would be no more.

The first coming pales in comparison to the second;
The first He was accompanied by palm branches,
The second by the armies of heaven.

"He is clothed with a robe dipped in blood."
Not the blood of anyone from above.
"His name is called the Word of God."

The unrepentant were trampled down;

You may look for them
But they won't be found.

A new sound is coming to the earth,
One we've never heard;
Some will hear God's thunder
And some will hear God's word.

Scripture referenced: John 12:19 (AMP), John 12:24, Psalm 118:26, Revelation 19:13

I Will Be Ready

I will be ready when the Lord returns.
I have set my mind to learn;
Learn of the Creator's existence.
To praise Jesus is an inbuilt persistence.

No easy thing to humble oneself like a child.
No easy thing to believe in someone
you won't see for a while.

Jesus is King,
His army will win.
Turn from the ways of the world,
Open your heart, let Him in.

"The world is passing away."
We don't have a say.
The only way to live forever,
Accept Jesus Christ today.

"Lord of lords and King of kings."
It is to Him my heart will sing.

He is the One who made me.
He is the One who saved me.
Without Him I'd be no more use than an aborted baby.
Abortion is murder,
Can we push God any further?

I'm not out here for the glory of man.
I'm here to fulfil God's plan.
His plan for my life,
He has one for you too;
Look to Jesus, all things will be made new.

Trusting in yourself will only lead you astray.
There's only one way to see it through;
Put your faith in Jesus Christ,
Why not do it today?

Scripture referenced: 1 John 2:17, Revelation 17:14, 1 Corinthians 7:31

LOVE IS PATIENT

Love is patient.
Love is kind.
Made possible by keeping Jesus
On your mind.

The economy is collapsing,
It is no accident.
When all is said and done
God's army will have won.

A crisis in the economy.
A crisis in our souls.
Put your faith in Jesus Christ,
You'll have confidence as you grow old.

Confidence that death is not the end.
Confidence that your soul will transcend,
Transcend beyond this world into your home called heaven;
It creates excitement like you had when you were eleven.

"The silver is mine
And the gold is mine,
Declares the Lord of Hosts."
Jesus is the one with the most.

The most wisdom.
The most love.

Love Is Patient

He willingly left His divine home up above.

The source of love.
The source of life.
His name is Jesus Christ.
He made all things right.

He died for you
And He died for me.
One day those who believe
Will live in heaven happily.

Scripture referenced: Haggai 2:8

All the World Will See

I will proclaim His name here today.
Jesus has paved the way;
The way for a blessed life,
One free from strife.

A blessed life,
One without fear or fright.
"A spirit of power, love and self-control."
Jesus will steal the show.

Satan's had his years of control,
Now it's time to let go.
Let go of old norms,
Let go of old systems,
Jesus is about to fix them.

He'll start with the finances
And move His hand right through the branches;
The branches of corrupt government,
The branches of corrupt media.
A new day is dawning for the believer.

A day of abundance.
A day of peace.
A day of vindication,
All the world will see.

Faith comes through hearing
And hearing by the preaching.
The preaching of the Word;
Listen to my brothers and sisters,
Jesus will teach you your worth.

Scripture referenced: 2 Timothy 1:7

The New Reality

The world has changed forever.
We haven't been brought out here to look clever.
Jesus is King of the world.
Will you humble yourselves like little boys and girls?

Give thanks to the Maker of heaven and earth.
Only Jesus knows your true worth.
A new time on the earth has just been birthed.

The prophet and the preacher will walk hand in hand,
They will proclaim the gospel
All throughout the land.

The world was held in bondage,
By God's power it has been set free.
We were all slaves to the system
But now we'll have honest money.

The hour is now,
The hour is late,
When God moves His hand will you be able to take?

Take the weight of the new reality?
Or bear the burden of your own depravity?

"There is a sound of abundance of rain."
That's what the prophet of old said,

Right before things were about to change.

I'm talking of the prophet Elijah,
There was no messenger higher.
He gave the word of the Lord,
Shortly after Jezebel's body was thrown to the floor.

Scripture referenced: 1 Kings 18:41 (KJV)

Meditate in Your Heart

"Meditate in your heart upon your bed."
Consider the words that you've said.
"And be still, reflect on your sin and repent of your rebellion."
Jesus is faithful, He'll let you in.

"You have put joy in my heart."
From this world we will depart.
Though we see death and decay;
We will be in heaven someday.

"In peace I will both lie down and sleep."
In heaven's company we will keep.
"For you alone, O Lord,
Make me dwell in safety and confident trust."
To escape hellfire,
Faith in Jesus is a must.

Scripture referenced: Psalm 4:4,7,8 (AMP)

Never Stood a Chance

Kings, priests and prophets,
No demon can stop us.
Dominion over the earth, sky and sea.
Jesus Christ is our victory.

One day in the future
We'll all look back;
We'll give glory to God
For every failed enemy attack.

A thousand years to us,
One day to the Lord.
When times get tough I take a pause;
I see Jesus and hear heaven's thunderous applause.

Myriads upon myriads,
Bowed before God's feet.
When I make it home to heaven,
Every single one I'll meet.

The Mighty Man.
My Father's perfect plan.
The Lord looks down,
His eyes are over every land
– The Jezebels and Hamans never stood a chance.
*Scripture referenced: 2 Peter 3:8, Daniel 7:10,
Revelation 5:11*

NOTHING WILL STAY THE SAME

An outpouring of His rain,
Everything is about to change;
The glory of God revealed,
Nothing will stay the same.

An uprising of His prophets,
An anointing on His preachers;
When the final harvest comes in,
Blessed will be His teachers.

"His rod and His staff comfort me,"
Yes the road was bumpy.
When His wealth transfer comes,
I'll plant all kinds of trees.

"Then the woman fled into the wilderness
Where she had a place prepared by God,"
In the thousand year reign,
We'll be living in the countryside with the frogs.

Scripture referenced: Psalm 23:4, Revelation 12:6

Never Stood a Chance

Kings, priests and prophets,
No demon can stop us.
Dominion over the earth, sky and sea.
Jesus Christ is our victory.

One day in the future
We'll all look back;
We'll give glory to God
For every failed enemy attack.

A thousand years to us,
One day to the Lord.
When times get tough I take a pause;
I see Jesus and hear heaven's thunderous applause.

Myriads upon myriads,
Bowed before God's feet.
When I make it home to heaven,
Every single one I'll meet.

The Mighty Man.
My Father's perfect plan.
The Lord looks down,
His eyes are over every land
– The Jezebels and Hamans never stood a chance.
*Scripture referenced: 2 Peter 3:8, Daniel 7:10,
Revelation 5:11*

Nothing Will Stay the Same

An outpouring of His rain,
Everything is about to change;
The glory of God revealed,
Nothing will stay the same.

An uprising of His prophets,
An anointing on His preachers;
When the final harvest comes in,
Blessed will be His teachers.

"His rod and His staff comfort me,"
Yes the road was bumpy.
When His wealth transfer comes,
I'll plant all kinds of trees.

"Then the woman fled into the wilderness
Where she had a place prepared by God,"
In the thousand year reign,
We'll be living in the countryside with the frogs.

Scripture referenced: Psalm 23:4, Revelation 12:6

Deliver Me From Fantasy

Lord, deliver me from fantasy,
Bring me back into reality.
There's a war on for your mind.
Every believer's soul is divine.
"Arise, shine." Now is the time,
The prophetic clock will continue to unwind.
"The Lord rises upon you
And His glory appears over you."
These days will be remembered
As those that God made new.

He is our God.
Jesus is King.
At the end of all things,
"Every eye will see Him."

"Wisdom is vindicated by her deeds."
Many wrongly imprisoned will be set free.
Justice and liberty for all.
"Do you not know?"
We will judge the ones who fall.

Hidden inventions.
Unsolved crimes.
These day will be remembered
As those that God brought to life.

"And the time arrived when the
Saints took possession of the kingdom."
If you can believe it,
This is about to begin.

'Joel two heaven invasion.'
Wait and see what's in store,
You'll be overwhelmed with elation.
Expectation of the days ahead.
Many wicked people sentenced to death.

A time to reap the seeds that have been sown;
A time to step into abundance foretold.

Scripture referenced: Isaiah 60:1-2, Revelation 1:7,
Matthew 11:19,
1 Corinthians 6:3, Daniel 7:22

A Lush Green Valley

Here we are,
Fields of green from afar.
Chirping birds,
They know their worth.
A lush green valley,
A peaceful day,
The sun beams down,
Spring gives way.

The summer beckons,
A blessing from heaven.
The grass grows tall,
"Seedtime and harvest" forevermore.

Peace in my soul,
It will never grow old.
To live off the land,
How profound.

God made it that way,
God gave us today;
Carpe diem
– Seize the day.

Scripture referenced: Genesis 8:22

Kier is most active on Instagram/Facebook and recently released his first album 'Holy Spirit Inspired Poems' which is available on Spotify, Apple Music, iTunes, Amazon and YouTube.

Instagram: @kier_collins

Facebook: Kier Collins

If you've been inspired by these poems and believe in your heart that there is something more than just living paycheck to paycheck creating memories and for your name to be forgotten three generations down the line; I would encourage you to reach out to God and ask Him to reveal Himself to you through His Son Jesus. God does not judge by outward appearance but by the intentions of a person's heart. If you pray in sincerity 'God if you're real show me' He will answer. Jesus Christ is the only way to heaven as He is the Father's only begotten Son. Without accepting Jesus' blood sacrifice on the cross 2000 years ago no one can enter heaven, no matter how 'good' they think they've been. Heaven is such a perfect place because no sin at all exists there, no human being beyond the age of innocence (this age is unique to each child) is without sin. Only Jesus lived a human life without committing a single sin, this is why His blood sacrifice is the only way we can gain entry into heaven.

"For God so loved the world, that He gave His only begotten Son, that whoever believes in Him shall not perish, but have eternal life."

John 3:16

Recommended Books:

Kat Kerr – Revealing Heaven (1 and 2)

Donna Rigney – Divine Encounters

Donna Rigney – The Glory of God Revealed

It isn't live at the time of writing (June 2023) but Kier intends to create a web site where all of the works he creates will be in one place. It will be kiercollins.com

God bless you and thank you for reading.